Under the Cherry Tree

In the hum of the market there is money,
But under the cherry tree there is rest.

UNDER THE CHERRY TREE

Poems for children chosen by Cynthia Mitchell

With pictures by Satomi Ichikawa

William Collins Publishers, Inc.

New York and Cleveland

To my family

William Collins Publishers Inc. would like to thank the following for permission to reprint the poems in this book. All possible care has been taken to trace the ownership of every selection included and to make full acknowledgment for its use. If any errors have accidentally occurred, they will be corrected in subsequent editions, provided notification is sent to the publishers: "The Pasture" by Robert Frost from *The Poetry of Robert Frost* edited by Edward Connery Lathem. Copyright 1939, 1967, 1969 by Holt, Rinehart & Winston. Reprinted by permission of Holt, Rinehart and Winston Publishers. "Preludes I" by T.S. Eliot from *Collected Poems 1909-1962* by T.S. Eliot. Copyright 1936 by Harcourt Brace Jovanovich, Inc. Copyright 1963, 1964 by T.S. Eliot. Reprinted by permission of the publisher. "Allie" from *Country Sentiment* by Robert Graves. Copyright 1920 by Robert Graves, renewed 1947, 1975. Reprinted by permission of Curtis Brown, Ltd. "Moonlit Apples" from *The Collected Poems of John Drinkwater* by John Drinkwater. Reprinted by permission of Sidgwick and Jackson, Publishers. "On My Little Guitar" from *On My Old Ramkietjie* by C. Lewis Liepoldt. Reprinted by permission of Antony Delius. "Full Moon Rhyme" from *Collected Poems 1942-1970* by Judith Wright. Reprinted by permission of Angus and Robertson, Publishers. "A Sea Burden" by C. Fox Smith. Reprinted by permission of Methuen & Co. Ltd. "What's Upstairs?" by John Walsh. Reprinted by permission of Mrs A.M. Walsh. "The Train in the Night" by Elizabeth Riddell. Reprinted by permission of the author and Angus & Robertson, Publishers. "Time to go Home" from *The Blackbird in the Lilac* by James Reeves, published by Oxford University Press (1952). Reprinted by permission of the publisher. "Choosing" by Olive Dove. Reprinted by permission of the author. "In the Garden" from *Come Along* by Stanley Cook. Reprinted by permission of the author. "Cats" by Eleanor Farjeon from *The Children's Bells*. Copyright 1957 by Eleanor Farjeon. Reprinted by permission of Harold Ober Associates Incorporated. "The Rathlin Cradle Song" from *A Treasury of Irish Saints*. Reprinted by permission of the estate of John Irvine and the Dolmen Press. "Who rolled in the mud" by Michael Rosen from *Mind Your Own Business*. Reprinted by permission of Andre Deutsch Ltd.

First published in the United States of America by William Collins Publishers, Inc. New York and Cleveland, 1979. This selection copyright © 1979 by Cynthia Mitchell. Illustrations copyright © 1979 by Satomi Ichikawa. (First published in Great Britain by William Heinemann Ltd., 1979)
Printed in Great Britain.

Library of Congress Cataloging in Publication Data
Main entry under title:
Under the cherry tree.
SUMMARY: An illustrated collection of poems on topics including spring pastures, twilight, and sleeping cats.
  1. Children's poetry. [1. Poetry—Collections]
I. Ichikawa, Satomi. II. Mitchell, Cynthia.
PN6109.97.U5 1979   808.81   79-11579
ISBN 0-529-05543-0
ISBN 0-529-05544-9 lib. bdg.

I'm going out to clean the pasture spring;
I'll only stop to rake the leaves away
(And wait to watch the water clear, I may):
I sha'n't be gone long.—You come too.

I'm going out to fetch the little calf
That's standing by the mother. It's so young
It totters when she licks it with her tongue.
I sha'n't be gone long.—You come too.

ROBERT FROST

Allie, call the birds in,
   The birds from the sky!
Allie calls, Allie sings,
   Down they all fly;
First there came
Two white doves,
   Then a sparrow from his nest,
Then a clucking bantam hen,
   Then a robin red-breast.

Allie, call the beasts in,
   The beasts, every one!
Allie calls, Allie sings,
   In they all run:
First there came
Two black lambs,
   Then a grunting Berkshire sow,
Then a dog without a tail,
   Then a red and white cow.

Allie, call the fish up,
  The fish from the stream!
Allie calls, Allie sings,
  Up they all swim:
First there came
Two gold fish,
  A minnow and a miller's thumb,
Then a school of little trout,
  Then the twisting eels come.

Allie, call the children,
  Call them from the green!
Allie calls, Allie sings,
  Soon they run in:
First there came
Tom and Madge,
  Kate and I who'll not forget
How we played by the water's edge
  Till the April sun set.

ROBERT GRAVES

Time to go home!
   Says the great steeple clock.
Time to go home!
   Says the gold weathercock.
Down sinks the sun
   In the valley to sleep;
Lost are the orchards
   In blue shadows deep.
Soft falls the dew
   On cornfield and grass;

Through the dark trees
    The evening airs pass:
Time to go home,
    They murmur and say;
Birds to their homes
    Have all flown away.
Nothing shines now
    But the gold weathercock.
Time to go home!
    Says the great steeple clock.

JAMES REEVES

It is the evening hour,
How silent all doth lie,
The hornèd moon he shows his face
In the river with the sky.
Just by the path on which we pass
The flaggy lake lies still as glass.

JOHN CLARE

A bonfire smoky and hazy,
When the flames have become quite lazy,
Is when I like it best of all.
The wood is all red and glowing
And into the embers are going
Chestnuts to roast for us all.

DAPHNE LISTER

The winter evening settles down
With smell of steaks in passageways.
Six o'clock.
The burnt-out ends of smoky days.
And now a gusty shower wraps
The grimy scraps
Of withered leaves about your feet
And newspapers from vacant lots;
The showers beat
On broken blinds and chimney-pots,
And at the corner of the street
A lonely cab-horse steams and stamps.
And then the lighting of the lamps.

T. S. ELIOT

A ship swinging,
As the tide swings, up and down,
And men's voices singing,
    East away O! West away!
    And a very long way from London Town.

A lantern glowing
And the stars looking down,
And the sea smells blowing.
    East away O! West away!
    And a very long way from London Town.

Lights in wild weather
From a tavern window, old and brown,
And men singing together,
    East away O! West away!
    And a very long way from London Town.

C. FOX SMITH

In the garden in winter
One rose
Like a creamy ice cream cornet
Still grows.

In the garden in winter
Two pears
That ripened all summer
Still hang there.

In the garden in winter
Three birds
Peck each other
And the bread.

In the garden in winter
Four trees
With leafless boughs
Comb the breeze.

In the garden in winter
Five cabbages grow
And wait to be eaten
In a row.

In the garden in winter
Six steps of stone
Are the only things
That don't feel cold.

In the garden in winter
Seven days of the week
Beneath the ground
The flower bulbs sleep.

STANLEY COOK

Who rolled in the mud
behind the garage door?
Who left footprints
across the kitchen floor?

I know a dog whose nose is cold
I know a dog whose nose is cold

Who chased raindrops
down the windows?
Who smudged the glass
with the end of his nose?

I know a dog with a cold in his nose
I know a dog with a cold in his nose

Who wants a bath
and a tuppenny ha'penny biscuit?
Who wants to bed down
in his fireside basket?

Me, said Ranzo
I'm the dog with a cold.

MICHAEL ROSEN

Cats sleep
Anywhere,
Any table,
Any chair,
Top of piano,
Window-ledge,
In the middle,
On the edge,

Open drawer,
Empty shoe,
Anybody's
Lap will do,
Fitted in a
Cardboard box,
In the cupboard
With your frocks—
Anywhere!
They don't care!
Cats sleep
Anywhere.

ELEANOR FARJEON

What's upstairs?...
The streets are still;
Outside the sun
Is gone from the hill.
I sit with mother:
The soft night airs
Creep into the house.
And what's upstairs?

Upstairs is my bedroom,
My chest-of-drawers,
My books, my paints,
My bottle of flowers.

And my bed will be bathed
In the shine of the moon
All the long long night . . .
And I'm going there soon.

JOHN WALSH

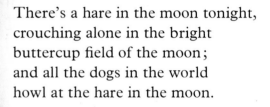

There's a hare in the moon tonight,
crouching alone in the bright
buttercup field of the moon;
and all the dogs in the world
howl at the hare in the moon.

"I chased that hare to the sky,"
the hungry dogs all cry.
"The hare jumped into the moon
and left me here in the cold.
I chased that hare to the moon."

"Come down again, mad hare,
we can see you there,"
the dogs all howl to the moon.
"Come down again to the world,
you mad black hare in the moon,

"or we will grow wings and fly
up to the star-grassed sky
to hunt you out of the moon,"
the hungry dogs of the world
howl at the hare in the moon.

JUDITH WRIGHT

Starlight, star bright,
First star I've seen tonight;
I wish I may, I wish I might
Get the wish I wish tonight.

TRADITIONAL

What do you choose?
Coral beads on a string,
Purple velvet and lace
And an emerald ring.

What will you have?
Pomegranates and pears,
Jellies, trifles and truffles
And chocolate eclairs.

What would you like?
A brown pony to ride
And three tiger-striped cats
To sleep at my side.

What is for you?
A palace fit for kings
With a grove of silver trees
Where a golden bird sings.

What is your wish?
To live by a storm tossed sea
In a lone grey tower
And hear the waves roaring hungrily.

OLIVE DOVE

On my little guitar
With only one string
I play in the moonlight
Any old thing.

C. LOUIS LEIPOLDT (*translated by A. Delius*)

Have you heard of the man
  Who stood on his head,
And put his clothes
  Into his bed,
And folded himself
  On a chair instead?

TRADITIONAL

The night is on the dark sea wave
And the boats are on the deep,
But here within the quiet room
My treasure lies asleep.
Oh! may Our Lady come and bless
The cradle where you lie,
And wind and wave, and moon and
      stars,
Shall sing you lullaby.

The woodland birds are silent now,
And the empty fields are still.
Night in her sable vestment walks
Across the lonely hill.
Oh! may Our Lady stoop to rock
The cradle where you lie,
And wind and wave, and moon and
        stars,
Shall sing you lullaby.

JOHN IRVINE

Who hears in the night
The train's sharp whistle
Cut off the top
Of chickweed and thistle
Flutter the birds
That drowse in the willow
And rouse the boy
From his frosty pillow?

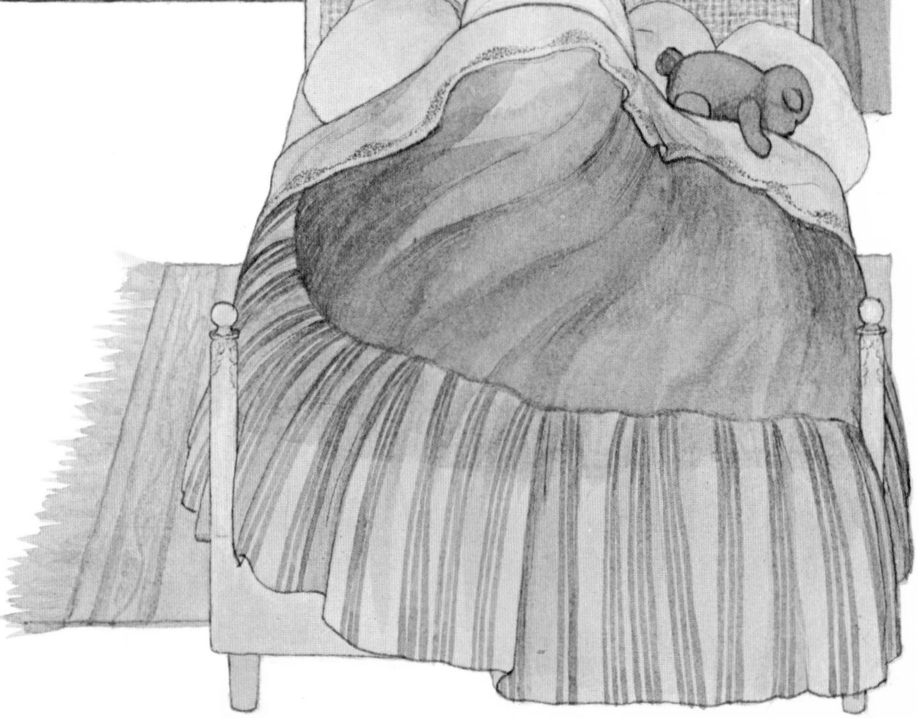

Who hears in the night
The wheels that mutter
Past mill and grave
Past barn and shutter
Is the boy for whom
All time unravels
Who'll swallow the wind
And go on his travels.

ELIZABETH RIDDELL

At the top of the house the apples are laid in rows,
And the skylight lets the moonlight in, and those
Apples are deep-sea apples of green. There goes
   A cloud on the moon in the autumn night.

A mouse in the wainscot scratches, and scratches, and then
There is no sound at the top of the house of men
Or mice; and the cloud is blown, and the moon again
   Dapples the apples with deep-sea light.

They are lying in rows there, under the gloomy beams;
On the sagging floor; they gather the silver streams
Out of the moon, those moonlit apples of dreams,
   And quiet is the steep stair under.

In the corridors under there is nothing but sleep.
And stiller than ever on orchard boughs they keep
Tryst with the moon, and deep is the silence, deep
   On moon-washed apples of wonder.

JOHN DRINKWATER

On his little twig of plum,
His plum-tree twig, the nightingale
Dreamed one night that snow had come,
On the hill and in the vale,
In the vale and on the hill,
Everything white and soft and still,
Only the snowflakes falling, falling,
Only the snow . . . .

On a night when the snow had come,
As the snowflakes fell the nightingale
Dreamed of orchards white with plum,
On the hill and in the vale,
In the vale and on the hill,
Everything white and soft and still,
Only the petals falling, falling,
Only the plum . . . .

IAN COLVIN (*translated from the Japanese*)